Table of Contents

Introduction

Purpose of the Manual

The purpose of this manual is to help you prepare to take the Special Agent Test. This manual will familiarize you with the Logical Reasoning Test, the Arithmetic Reasoning Test, and the Writing Skills Test and will give you a chance to study some sample questions and explanations for the correct answers to each question. If you have not had much practice taking written, multiple-choice tests, you will have an opportunity to see what the tests look like and to practice taking questions similar to those on the tests.

Organization of the Manual

The manual is organized into four sections. The first section provides some tips for taking the Special Agent Test. The second section provides preparation material for the Logical Reasoning Test and includes a practice test with explanations for the answers to the practice test. The third section provides preparation material for the Arithmetic Reasoning Test and includes a practice test with explanations for the answers to the practice test. Finally, the fourth section provides preparation material for the Writing Skills Test and includes a practice test with explanations for the answers to the practice test.

Section I
Test Taking Tips

1. You will do your best on the test if you stay calm and relaxed. Take a few deep, slow breaths to help you maintain your calm.

2. Pay careful attention to all directions before beginning.

3. Answer the easier questions first. Skip questions you find to be very difficult and come back to them later.

4. For each question, read the entire question and all response options carefully before deciding upon an answer.

5. If you do not know the answer to a question, eliminate the response options that you know to be incorrect or probably incorrect and then guess from the remaining response options.

6. Your score is based only on the number of questions you answer correctly. You are not penalized for answering questions incorrectly. Therefore, you should answer every question, even questions that you must guess.

7. If you finish before time is up, go back and check your answers.

8. Be sure that you mark your answer sheet correctly. If you have to change an answer, erase the first answer before marking the new answer. If you skip a question, be sure to answer the next question in the appropriate place on the answer sheet.

9. Ignore any patterns of A's, B's, C's, D's, or E's on your answer sheet. These correct answer positions are chosen randomly and there is no way to improve your chances by guessing based on an answer sheet pattern.

Section II Preparing for the Logical Reasoning Test

Introduction

Purpose of this Section

The purpose of this section is to help you prepare to take the Logical Reasoning Test. The test described in this section evaluates how well applicants can read, understand, and apply critical thinking skills to factual situations. Special Agents must read and study laws, legal commentary, and regulations. They often must make critical decisions that require superior reasoning skills. Additionally, they may be called upon to testify in court and must be able to follow and anticipate the kind of reasoning used in legal proceedings. As a result, they will receive training at the Federal Law Enforcement Training Center that requires that they read, understand, and be able to apply a wealth of detailed, written information. Although some information must be memorized, much of the information that Special Agents will use must be learned through independent reasoning. This test is designed to select trainees who will be able to handle the very demanding academic workload at the training academy and who will subsequently be able to handle complex reasoning and decision-making situations on the job.

This section of the manual will familiarize you with the test and the instructions and will give you a chance to study some sample questions and explanations for the correct answers to each question. You will have an opportunity to see what the test looks like and to practice taking questions similar to those on the test.

Educated Guessing

There is no penalty for guessing on this test; therefore, you should answer every question. If you guess blindly, you have one chance in five of getting the right answer. However, your chance of choosing the right answer just by guessing is greatly improved by using a little mental detective work to eliminate one or more response options that are probably or certainly wrong.

A poor guessing strategy is to try to determine the next answer based on its letter or on some pattern of letters among the answer choices. There may be several D's or A's or any other letter in a row, or there may not be. Trying to uncover some pattern in these letters and guessing based on that pattern is not an effective test-taking strategy.

Preparing For Logical Reasoning Questions

Logical Reasoning

Reasoning is the single most important competency for successful performance in the Special Agent job. Correct reasoning is useful for decision-making and problem solving, activities that prevail on the job. In this part, you will read some useful information about reasoning correctly.

The questions in this examination are designed to test your ability to understand complicated written material and to derive correct conclusions from it. The kind of reading that these questions ask you to do is different from ordinary reading in which you just follow the general meaning of a series of sentences to see what the writer thinks about a topic. It is the kind of reading you have to do with complex material when you intend to take some action or draw some conclusion based on that material.

The test asks you to make logical conclusions based on facts you are given in various paragraphs. These conclusions need to be based only on the facts in the paragraph. Therefore, answering requires careful reading and focused thought about what information is given and what information is <u>not</u> given.

The following information will give you some suggestions about how to approach the questions and some information about how you can develop your reasoning skills.

Reading the Paragraph

Every reading paragraph in the test is drawn from some kind of written material relating to Special Agent or Government work. There may be facts in a paragraph that do not actually apply to every part of the Federal Government or that may not always be true everywhere. In answering the questions, it is important that you **accept every fact in the paragraph as true**. Remember that you are not being judged on your knowledge of facts, but rather on your ability to read and reason on the basis of given facts.

Not all information is of the same type. There can be information about events and there can be information about groups (or categories) of things. Information can also be positive or negative. Usually, information is positive (for example, "these tire tracks are several days old"), but knowledge that something is <u>not</u> the case is also useful information (for example, "these tire tracks are <u>not</u> from a truck").

Reading the Lead-In or Basic Question

In this test, you will find a paragraph, followed by a lead-in phrase that asks you to complete a sentence by choosing one of several response options labeled from (A) to (E). The lead-in phrase may be either positive or negative:

> *"From the information given above, it can be validly concluded that"*

or

> *"From the information given above, it CANNOT be validly concluded that"*

It is important to focus on the lead-in phrase at the beginning of a question to determine whether it is positive or negative. Do not skim over the lead-in phrase.

Positive lead-in phrases are followed by four invalid conclusions and one valid conclusion. Your task is to find the valid one. Negative lead-in phrases, by contrast, are followed by four valid conclusions and only one invalid conclusion. The task in these questions is to determine what **cannot** be validly concluded based on the facts in the paragraph.

The lead-in phrase may also limit the possible answers in some way. For example, a lead-in phrase such as *"From the information given above, it can be validly concluded that, <u>during the 1990's in California</u>"* means that there might be different answers based on other times and places, but for the purpose of the test question, only conditions in California during the 1990's (as described in the paragraph) should be considered.

Reasoning About Groups or Categories

As was stated before, not all information is of the same type. There can be information about events or situations, and there can be information about individuals and groups (or categories). Next, we discuss how to deal with information about groups or categories.

"All" Statements

A statement about two groups that begins with the words "all" or "every" gives you some important information about how the two groups are related. The words "all" and "every" tell you that everything in the first group is also in the second group. For example, in the statement, "All the law enforcement officers on the case are Federal law enforcement officers," the first group, consisting of law enforcement officers on the case, is totally included in the second group, consisting of Federal law enforcement officers.

"All" and "Every" are KEY WORDS that signify important information about how two groups are related.

The "all" statement does not provide sufficient information to determine whether or not all members of the second group are included in the first group. Suppose that a librarian told you "All the books on this set of shelves are about law enforcement." From this information, you might be tempted to conclude that all of the library's books on law enforcement (the second group) are on that set of shelves (the first group), but this conclusion is invalid. The books on those shelves might only be part of the entire group of books on law enforcement. The sentence does NOT provide information on whether or not other law enforcement books are placed elsewhere in the library. The following examples provide an "all" statement (all of Group A are Group B) followed by an invalid "all" statement (all of Group B are Group A). To develop a good grasp of this concept, try to create some examples of your own.

Table 1: Invalid Conclusions from "All" statements

True:	All the people at my party speak Spanish.
Invalid Conclusion:	All the people who speak Spanish are at my party.
True:	All Supreme Court justices are lawyers.
Invalid Conclusion:	All lawyers are Supreme Court justices.
True:	All U.S. Presidents were elected officials.
Invalid Conclusion:	All officials who were elected are U.S. Presidents.

Table 1, continued	
True:	Every ICE Special Agent works for the U.S. Government.
Invalid Conclusion:	Everyone working for the U.S. Government is an ICE Special Agent.
True:	Every U.S. Senator is a member of the U.S. Congress.
Invalid Conclusion:	Every member of the U.S. Congress is a U.S. Senator.

Every "all" statement provides sufficient information to determine that at least some members of the second group are included in the first group. Returning to our previous examples, we can validly conclude that "some Federal law enforcement officers are on the case" and that "some of the books about law enforcement are on this set of shelves." Developing numerous examples on your own of a true "all" statement (all of Group A are Group B) and a "some" statement (some of Group B are Group A) will help you to develop a mastery of this concept.

Table 2: Valid Conclusions from "All" Statements	
True:	All the people at my party speak Spanish.
Valid Conclusion:	Some people who speak Spanish are at my party.
True:	All Supreme Court justices are lawyers.
Valid Conclusion:	Some lawyers are Supreme Court justices.
True:	All U.S. Presidents were elected officials.
Valid Conclusion:	Some officials who were elected are U.S. Presidents.
True:	Every ICE Special Agent works for the U.S. Government.
Valid Conclusion:	Some employees of the U.S. Government are ICE Special Agents.
True:	Every U.S. Senator is a member of the U.S. Congress.
Valid Conclusion:	Some members of the U.S. Congress are U.S. Senators.

Reasoning From "None" and "Not" Statements

Information that something is **NOT** true is useful information. For example, you may learn that one group of things is **NOT** part of another group of things. This is the same as saying that there is no overlap at all between the two groups of things. Here, you can draw conclusions about either group as it relates to the other since you can count on the fact that the two groups have no members in common. If you can say that none of the stolen cars recovered from the rail yards were cars stolen from Canada, you can **also** say that none of the cars stolen from Canada were recovered from the rail yards because you know that the first statement means that there is no overlap between the two groups. In the test, you will see phrases or terms such as "It is not the case that" or "Not all of" or words that begin with the prefix "non-." All of these are ways to say that a negative fact has been established.

"No" and "not" are KEY WORDS that signify important information about how two groups are related.

Sometimes, our ordinary speech habits can cause us to jump to conclusions. Most people would not make a statement such as "Some of the pizza has no pepperoni" unless they are trying to suggest at the same time that some of the pizza does have pepperoni. By contrast, a detective might make a statement such as "some of the bloodstains were not human blood" simply because only part of the samples had come back from the laboratory. The detective is trying to suggest that at least some of the bloodstains were not human blood. The rest of the bloodstains might or might not be human blood.

As you work through the practice test, think about each negative phrase or term you find. Take care to assume only as much as is definitely indicated by the facts as given, and no more.

Reasoning About Parts of a Group

The term "some" refers to a part of a larger group. For example, in the statement "Some Special Agents are taking specialized training," the term "some Special Agents" refers to a portion of the group of all Special Agents. You should note, however, that the fact that we know that "some Special Agents are taking specialized training" implies nothing about the remaining portion of the set of Special Agents: other Special Agents may or may not be taking specialized training. Unless information is provided in the paragraph to the contrary, treat "some" as meaning "at least some."

Statements that refer to a portion of a set may contain other terms such as "most," "a few," or "almost all." Also, as discussed in the previous section, they can be negative, as in "Many Special Agents are not fluent in French." From this statement you may be tempted to infer that there are at least a few Special Agents who are fluent in French, but that would be jumping to a conclusion. From this statement alone, you do not know about the entire group of Special Agents and whether or not they are fluent in French. In these cases, you should remember that the term refers only to a part of the group and that from this information on part of the group you cannot infer anything about the rest of the group. Neglecting this principle of sound reasoning can cause costly errors.

> Unless information is provided in the paragraph to the contrary, treat "some" as meaning "at least some."

When you see a paragraph describing parts of a group, read the paragraph carefully to see if that description is based on knowledge of the entire group or only on knowledge of part of the group.

Reasoning About "If-Then" Statements

As was said before, there can be information about events or situations, and there can be information about individuals and groups. Previously, we discussed how to deal with information about groups. Next, we discuss how to deal with information about the relationship between events or situations.

We are all familiar with the idea of a cause and effect in which one thing leads to another thing, which in turn leads to a third thing, and so on. For example, "if a financial institution suspects that a deposit of funds stems from criminal activity, the institution is required to report the deposit transaction to the authorities." In this example, a suspicious deposit is a cause and the institution reporting the deposit is the effect.

Cause and effect means that when the first thing happens, the later event MUST follow. For example, if First Salem Bank suspects that Mr. Tubill deposited funds stemming from criminal activity, First Salem Bank is required to report Mr. Tubill's deposit to the authorities.

The cause and effect relationship also informs you that if the effect never occurred, the cause MUST NOT have occurred. For example, if First Salem Bank is NOT required to report Mr. Tubill's deposit to the authorities, then First Salem Bank does NOT suspect that Mr. Tubill deposited funds stemming from criminal activity.

The wording we typically use to indicate this kind of cause and effect linkage between events includes the simple "if-then" sentence in which the first event is in a statement tagged by "if" and the second event is in a statement tagged by "then." The "if-then" statement can also be used to express relationships other than the cause and effect relationship. Permission is sometimes expressed using the "if-then" statement. For instance, if an individual wishes to open a checking account anonymously, the individual may not open the account. Obligation is also sometimes expressed using the "if-then" statement. For example, if an officer places an individual under arrest, the arrestee must be provided with Miranda warnings.

What cause and effect, permission, and obligation all have in common is that they relate one event or situation to another event or situation. In this relationship, two things are always true. First, whenever the first event or situation occurs, the second event or situation MUST occur. Second, whenever the second event or situation has not occurred, then the first event or situation MUST NOT have occurred.

"If" and "Whenever" signify that important information is presented.

It is important to realize that the relationship expressed by any "if-then" statement works in one direction only: the converse of the "if-then" statement is invalid. For example, you learn that "If the jet engines are reversed, then the speed of the plane will decrease very rapidly." This sentence does NOT mean that the only possible cause of the plane decreasing speed very rapidly is that the jet engines are reversed. Therefore, from this information you cannot validly infer the converse statement, "If the speed of the plane decreases very rapidly, then the jet engines have been reversed." There might be some other cause for the speed of the plane to decrease rapidly. The following examples start with a true "if-then" sentence, followed by an invalid "if-then" sentence with the relationship of the first and second statements conversed.

Table 3: Invalid Conclusions from "If-Then" Statements	
True: Invalid Conclusion:	If a person is an ICE Special Agent, the person is an employee of the U.S. Government. If a person is an employee of the U.S. Government, the person is an ICE Special Agent.
True: Invalid Conclusion:	If a criminal receives a pardon, the criminal will be released. If a criminal is released, the criminal has received a pardon.
True: Invalid Conclusion:	If a person is convicted of murder, that person is guilty of a felony. If a person is guilty of a felony, that person has been convicted of murder.
True: Invalid Conclusion:	If a person lives in Germany, the person lives in Europe. If a person lives in Europe, the person lives in Germany.
True: Invalid Conclusion:	If a car has no gas, the car will not run. If a car does not run, the car has no gas.

Whenever the second event or situation has not occurred, then the first event or situation MUST NOT have occurred. This means that you can validly converse the relationship of these two statements as long as the statements are negated (made opposite). For example, you learn that "If the jet engines are reversed (the first statement), the speed of the plane will decrease very rapidly (the second statement)." Given that the information is true, it cannot be the case that the jet engines are reversed but the speed of the plane does not decrease very rapidly. Therefore, you can validly infer that "If the speed of the plane does not decrease very rapidly (the negation or opposite of the second statement), then the jet engines have not been reversed" (the negation or opposite of the first statement). The following examples start with a true "if-then" sentence, followed by a true (or valid) "if-then" sentence with the relationship of the first and second statements conversed and the statements themselves made opposite (negated).

Table 4: Valid Conclusions from "If-Then" Statements	
True:	If a person is an ICE Special Agent, the person is an employee of the U.S. Government.
Valid Conclusion	If a person is not an employee of the U.S. Government, the person is not an ICE Special Agent.
True:	If a criminal receives a pardon, the criminal will be released.
Therefore, True:	If a criminal is not released, the criminal has not received a pardon.
True:	If a person is convicted of murder, that person is guilty of a felony.
Therefore, True:	If a person is not guilty of a felony, that person has not been convicted of murder.
True:	If a person lives in Germany, the person lives in Europe.
Therefore, True:	If a person does not live in Europe, the person does not live in Germany.
True:	If a car has no gas, the car will not run.
Therefore, True:	If a car runs, the car has gas.

When the effect in a cause and effect relationship has not happened, the cause must not have happened.

As was said before, you can infer the opposite of the first statement from the opposite of the second statement. However, you cannot infer the opposite of the second statement from the opposite of the first statement. For example, you cannot validly infer that "If the jet engines are not reversed (the opposite of the first statement), then the speed of the plane does not decrease very rapidly" (the opposite of the second statement). The following examples start with a true "if-then" sentence followed by an invalid "if-then" sentence in which the first and second statements have been made opposite.

Table 5: More Invalid Conclusions from "If-Then" Statements

True:	If a person is an ICE Special Agent, the person is an employee of the U.S. Government.
Invalid Conclusion:	If a person is not an ICE Special Agent, the person is not an employee of the U.S. Government.
True:	If a criminal receives a pardon, the criminal will be released.
Invalid Conclusion:	If a criminal does not receive a pardon, the criminal will not be released.
True:	If a person is convicted of murder, that person is guilty of a felony.
Invalid Conclusion:	If a person is not convicted of murder, that person is not guilty of a felony.
True:	If a person lives in Germany, the person lives in Europe.
Invalid Conclusion:	If a person does not live in Germany, the person does not live in Europe.
True:	If a car has no gas, the car will not run.
Invalid Conclusion:	If a car has gas, the car will run.

A Few Final Cautions About Wording

There are test preparation classes that train people to take tests. In some of these classes, students are advised against choosing any answer in a reasoning test if it starts with the word "all" or the word "none." This is supposed to be useful advice because it is believed that most correct answers strike a balance between extremes and usually do not cover subjects that can be summarized in sentences beginning with "all" or "none." If you have heard this advice before, you should ignore it for this test. "All" statements and "none" statements occur in real-life situations and, consequently, you will be asked to work with them in this test in the reading paragraphs as well as in both correct and incorrect responses.

In general, you should pay attention to any words that provide information on groups or on linked events. This includes a wide range of negative words (such as "seldom" or "never" or "illegal" or "prohibited") and negative prefixes (such as "non-" "un-" or "dis-"). It also includes positive words (such as "all" or "some" or "most" or "always"). You should also watch for connectors such as "whenever" or "unless" or "except," since these words sometimes contain key information about relations among the facts given in the paragraph.

> Look for KEY WORDS such as "all," "some," "none," and "if" and for negative prefixes such as "non-," "un-," or "dis-."

English is a language that ordinarily uses single negatives. The word "not," by itself, does the job of making a formal English sentence into its opposite: "That bird is NOT an eagle." On this test, if you read a sentence such as "The cord is not wound," it means the cord is still unwound. When an English sentence has two negatives, the sentence has a positive meaning. For example, a sentence that reads "This application is NOT unworthy" means that the application IS worthy. The sentence "The bell did ring" could be stated, "It is NOT the case that the bell did NOT ring."

Finally, it is extremely important to pay close attention to the use of the word "ONLY." A sentence such as "The door will open IF AND ONLY IF both keys are used" is a very strong statement that means that there is just one way to open the door—with both keys. If the sentence just said, "The door will open if the key is used," there may be several other ways to open the door. But that is not the case when the expression "if and only if" is used.

Drawing Probabilistic Conclusions

When working on cases, Special Agents frequently must make decisions and draw conclusions that have some probability of being true, but they are not definitely true. On the test, there are questions that ask you to apply this type of logic. In each of the questions of this type, you will be presented with a paragraph of information and five response options. Your task is to select the response option that can be validly concluded from the information given in the paragraph. Use only the information provided in the paragraph. Do not speculate or make assumptions that go beyond this information. Also, assume that all information given in the paragraph is true, even if it conflicts with some fact that is known to you. Keep in mind that each question has only one correct answer.

When you have information about a group, you can apply that information to an individual member of that group with a degree of certainty. In other words, you can establish the probability that the information you have about the group applies to a single member of the group. For example, if most felons are repeat offenders and K.B. is a felon, then you can conclude that K.B. is most likely a repeat offender.

In order to establish a numerical probability, you must have information about the entire group. Although it may not be immediately obvious, percentages provide information about an entire group.

For example, if you know that 30% of all Special Agents have led a fraud investigation, you know that **only** 30% of Special Agents have led a fraud investigation. The percentage does not mean that at least 30% of Special Agents have led a fraud investigation. Because only 30% percent have led such an investigation, you know that the remaining Special Agents have **not** led a fraud investigation. Therefore, of all Special Agents, 70% (100% - 30% = 70%) have not led a fraud investigation. The entire group of Special Agents has been accounted for: 30% have led a fraud investigation and 70% have not.

Speaking more abstractly, we are dealing with statements about two groups in which a percentage is used to modify the first group. The percentage tells us that a portion of the first group is included in the second group, but the remainder of the first group is not included in the second group. Thus, the entire first group is accounted for. The following examples start with a true statement expressing something about a portion of a group using a percentage, followed by a true statement expressing the opposite about the remaining portion of the group.

Table 6: Valid Probabilistic Conclusions	
True:	Of all Government employees, 5% work for the Department of Justice.
Therefore, True:	Of all Government employees, 95% do not work for the Department of Justice.
True:	Eighty-five percent of state criminals did not receive parole.
Therefore, True:	Fifteen percent of state criminals received parole.
True:	Of all the visa applications, 10% were denied.
Therefore, True:	Of all the visa applications, 90% were not denied.

To determine a probability, you apply the information about the group to an individual member of the group. For example, if you pick one of the Special Agents at random, your chances of picking one who has led a fraud investigation is equal to the percentage of Special Agents who have led such an investigation. Because 30% of all Special Agents have led a fraud investigation, you can conclude that any particular Special Agent has a 30% chance of having led such an investigation. Furthermore, if you pick one of the Special Agents at random, your chances of picking one who has not led a fraud investigation is equal to the percentage of Special Agents who have not led such an investigation. You can validly conclude that any particular Special Agent has a 70% chance of not having led a fraud investigation because 70% of all Special Agents have not led a fraud investigation. The following examples start with a true statement about a group, followed by two valid statements expressing probability about an individual member of the group.

To determine a probability, you apply the information about the group to an individual member of the group.

Table 7: More Valid Probabilistic Conclusions	
True:	Of all Government employees, 5% work for the Department of Justice.
Therefore, True:	There is a 5% chance that a Government employee chosen at random works for the Department of Justice.
Therefore, True:	There is a 95% chance that a Government employee chosen at random does not work for the Department of Justice.

Table 7, Continued	
True:	Eighty-five percent of state criminals did not receive parole.
Therefore, True:	There is an 85% chance that a state criminal chosen at random did not receive parole.
Therefore, True:	There is a 15% chance that a state criminal chosen at random received parole.
True:	Of all the visa applications, 10% were denied.
Therefore, True:	There is a 10% chance that a visa application chosen at random was denied.
Therefore, True:	There is a 90% chance that a visa application chosen at random was not denied.

We looked at two types of valid conclusions. These valid conclusions were based on applying the given percentage to a member of the first group. Now, let us look at two types of invalid conclusions. These invalid conclusions are based on mistakenly applying the given percentage to a member of the second group.

Remember that a statement about two groups that begins with the word "all" gives you information about how the two groups are related. The word "all" tells you that everything in the first group is also in the second group. However, the "all" statement does not provide sufficient information to determine whether or not all members of the second group are included in the first group. Likewise, statements that use a percentage to describe the first group do not provide sufficient information to determine the portion of members of the second group that are included in the first group.

Having information about the entire first group in the statement is not the same as having information about the entire second group. For example, knowing that 60% of Special Agents have captured a fugitive (and, thus, that 40% of them have not) is not the same as knowing that of everyone who has captured a fugitive, 60% are Special Agents. It may be the case that 60% of those who have captured a fugitive are Special Agents, but it might not be the case. There is insufficient information about the entire set of people who have captured a fugitive to make exact percentage determinations about them.

In these statements that relate two groups using a percentage, the percentage given only applies to one group. In our example, the percentage applies to the first group, Special Agents, not to the second group (namely, those who have captured a fugitive). The following examples start with a true statement followed by two invalid statements where the percentage is incorrectly applied to the second group.

Table 8: Invalid Probabilistic Conclusions	
True:	Of all Government employees, 5% work for the Department of Justice.
Invalid Conclusion:	Of all employees of the Department of Justice, 5% work for the Government.
Invalid Conclusion:	Of all employees of the Department of Justice, 95% do not work for the Government.
True:	Eighty-five percent of state criminals did not receive parole.
Invalid Conclusion:	Eighty-five percent of those who received parole were not state criminals.
Invalid Conclusion:	Fifteen percent of those who received parole were state criminals.
True:	Of all the visa applications, 10% were denied.
Invalid Conclusion:	Of all the denied applications, 10% were visa applications.
Invalid Conclusion:	Of all the denied applications, 90% were not visa applications.

Because the percentage applies to the first group, not the second group, any statement of probability that is based on applying the percentage to the second group is invalid. For example, there is insufficient information about those who have captured a fugitive to determine the probability that a person who has captured a fugitive is a Special Agent. Also, there is insufficient information to determine the probability that a person who has captured a fugitive is not a Special Agent. The following examples start with a true statement followed by two invalid statements where a probability is determined based on the inappropriate application of the percentage to the second group.

Table 8: More Invalid Probabilistic Conclusions	
True:	Of all Government employees, 5% work for the Department of Justice.
Invalid Conclusion:	An employee of the Department of Justice chosen at random has a 5% of working for the Government.
Invalid Conclusion:	An employee of the Department of Justice chosen at random has a 95% of not working for the Government.

Table 8, Continued	
True:	Eighty-five percent of state criminals did not receive parole.
Invalid Conclusion:	The chances are 85% that a person selected at random who received parole was not a state criminal.
Invalid Conclusion:	The chances are 15% that a person selected at random who received parole was a state criminal.
True:	Of all the visa applications, 10% were denied.
Invalid Conclusion:	The chances are 10% that a denied application chosen at random is a visa application.
Invalid Conclusion:	The chances are 90% that a denied application chosen at random is not a visa application.

Remember These Tips When Taking the Logical Reasoning Test

1. In questions with positive lead statements, always choose the only conclusion that can definitely be drawn from the information given in the paragraph.
2. Remember NOT to use any outside factual information to reach your conclusion.
3. Read the lead-in sentence and the paragraph very carefully. Also, read all the answer choices before you mark the one you think is correct.
4. Pay special attention whenever the question uses words such as "all," "some," or "none." Other terms such as "unless" or "except" or "only" are also important. These words help to define the facts from which you must draw conclusions.
5. Also pay special attention whenever you see a negative prefix such as "non-" or a negative verb such as "disconnect" or "unfasten." These may be crucial to understanding the basic facts in the paragraph.
6. Ignore any advice you may have received in the past about avoiding an answer that contains the word "all" or the word "none." These may be signs of an incorrect response in some tests, but not in this test. You will find these words in both right and wrong response options.
7. Take the sample test and study the explanation for each of the questions very carefully. This will help you fine-tune your reasoning on the actual test.

LOGICAL REASONING PRACTICE TEST

The practice test contains questions that are similar to, but not exactly the same as, the questions on the real test. The practice test is followed by detailed explanations of every practice test question. These explanations will give you information about what is correct about the correct response options and what is incorrect about the wrong response options. Understanding the reasons for the correct and incorrect response options should assist you in distinguishing between a right and wrong answer on the test.

PRACTICE TEST

In questions 1 through 10, some questions will ask you to select the only answer that can be validly concluded from the paragraph. These questions include a paragraph followed by five response options. Preceding the five response options will be the phrase "From the information given above, it can be validly concluded that." In other questions you may be asked to select the only answer that ***cannot*** *be validly concluded from the paragraph. These questions include a paragraph followed by five response options. Preceding the five response options will be the phrase "From the information given above, it* ***CANNOT*** *be validly concluded that."*

You must use ***only*** *the information provided in the paragraph, without using any outside information whatsoever.*

It is suggested that you take not more than 20 minutes to complete questions 1 through 10. The questions on this practice test will not be on the real test, but the real questions will be similar in form and difficulty to these. The explanations for the correct and incorrect responses are found after the sample questions.

1. Often, crimes are characterized as either *malum in se*—inherently evil—or *malum prohibitum*—criminal because they are declared as offenses by a legislature. Murder is an example of the former. Failing to file a tax return illustrates the latter. Some jurisdictions no longer distinguish between crimes *malum in se* and *malum prohibitum,* although many still do.

   From the information given above, it can be validly concluded that

   A) many jurisdictions no longer distinguish between crimes *malum in se* and *malum prohibitum*
   B) some jurisdictions still distinguish between crimes *malum in se* and *malum prohibitum*
   C) some crimes characterized as *malum in se* are not inherently evil
   D) some crimes characterized as *malum prohibitum* are not declared by a legislature to be an offense
   E) sometimes failing to file a tax return is characterized as *malum in se*

2. A trucking company can act as a *common carrier*—for hire to the general public at published rates. As a common carrier, it is liable for any cargo damage, unless the company can show that it was not negligent. If the company can demonstrate that it was not negligent, then it is not liable for cargo damage. In contrast, a *contract carrier* (a trucking company hired by a shipper under a specific contract) is only responsible for cargo damage as spelled out in the contract. A Claus Inc. tractor-trailer, acting under common carrier authority, was in a 5-vehicle accident that damaged its cargo. A Nichols Inc. tractor-trailer, acting under contract carrier authority, was involved in the same accident, and its cargo was also damaged.

   From the information given above, it can be validly concluded that, in reference to the accident,

   A) if Claus Inc. is liable, then it can show that it was not negligent
   B) if Claus Inc. cannot show that it was not negligent, then it is not liable
   C) if Claus Inc. can show that it was not negligent, then it is not liable
   D) if Nichols Inc. is liable, then it cannot show that it is negligent
   E) if Nichols Inc. can show that it is not negligent, then it is not liable

3. A rapidly changing technical environment in government is promoting greater reliance on electronic mail (e-mail) systems. As this usage grows, there are increasing chances of conflict between the users' expectations of privacy and public access rights. In some investigations, access to all e-mail, including those messages stored in archival files and messages outside the scope of the investigation, has been sought and granted. In spite of this, some people send messages through e-mail that would never be said face-to-face or written formally.

   From the information given above, it ***CANNOT*** *be validly concluded that*

   A) some e-mail messages that have been requested as part of investigations have contained messages that would never be said face-to-face
   B) some messages that people would never say face-to-face are sent in e-mail messages
   C) some e-mail messages have been requested as part of investigations
   D) e-mail messages have not been exempted from investigations
   E) some e-mail messages contain information that would be omitted from formal writing

4. Phyllis T. is a former Federal employee who was entitled to benefits under the Federal Employee Compensation Act because of a job-related, disabling injury. When an eligible Federal employee has such an injury, the benefit is determined by this test: If the beneficiary is married or has dependents, benefits are 3/4 of the person's salary at the time of the injury; otherwise, benefits are set at 2/3 of the salary. Phyllis T.'s benefits were 2/3 of her salary when she was injured.

   From the information given above, it can be validly concluded that, when Phyllis T. was injured, she

   A) was married but without dependents
   B) was not married and had no dependents
   C) was not married but had dependents
   D) was married and had dependents
   E) had never been married

5. Some 480,000 immigrants were living in a certain country in 1999. Although most of these immigrants were not employed in professional occupations, many of them were. For instance, many of them were engineers and many of them were nurses. Very few of these immigrants were librarians, another professional occupation.

   From the information given above, it can be validly concluded that, in 1999, in the country described above,

   A) most immigrants were either engineers or nurses
   B) it is not the case that some of the nurses were immigrants
   C) none of the engineers were immigrants
   D) most of those not employed in professional occupations were immigrants
   E) some of the engineers were immigrants

6. Police officers were led to believe that many weapons sold at a certain gun store were sold illegally. Upon investigating the lead, the officers learned that all of the weapons sold by the store that were made by Precision Arms were sold legally. Also, none of the illegally sold weapons were .45 caliber.

   From the information given above, it can be validly concluded that, concerning the weapons sold at the store,

   A) all of the .45 caliber weapons were made by Precision Arms
   B) none of the .45 caliber weapons were made by Precision Arms
   C) some of the weapons made by Precision Arms were .45 caliber weapons
   D) all of the .45 caliber weapons were sold legally
   E) some of the weapons made by Precision Arms were sold illegally

7. Impressions made by the ridges on the ends of the fingers and thumbs are useful means of identification, since no two persons have the same pattern of ridges. If finger patterns from fingerprints are not decipherable, then they cannot be classified by general shape and contour or by pattern type. If they cannot be classified by these characteristics, then it is impossible to identify the person to whom the fingerprints belong.

   *From the information given above, it **CANNOT** be validly concluded that*

   A) if it is possible to identify the person to whom fingerprints belong, then the fingerprints are decipherable
   B) if finger patterns from fingerprints are not decipherable, then it is impossible to identify the person to whom the fingerprints belong
   C) if fingerprints are decipherable, then it is impossible to identify the person to whom they belong
   D) if fingerprints can be classified by general shape and contour or by pattern type, then they are decipherable
   E) if it is possible to identify the person to whom fingerprints belong, then the fingerprints can be classified by general shape and contour or pattern type

8. Explosives are substances or devices capable of producing a volume of rapidly expanding gases that exert a sudden pressure on their surroundings. Chemical explosives are the most commonly used, although there are mechanical and nuclear explosives. All mechanical explosives are devices in which a physical reaction is produced, such as that caused by overloading a container with compressed air. While nuclear explosives are by far the most powerful, all nuclear explosives have been restricted to military weapons.

   From the information given above, it can be validly concluded that

   A) all explosives that have been restricted to military weapons are nuclear explosives
   B) no mechanical explosives are devices in which a physical reaction is produced, such as that caused by overloading a container with compressed air
   C) some nuclear explosives have not been restricted to military weapons
   D) all mechanical explosives have been restricted to military weapons
   E) some devices in which a physical reaction is produced, such as that caused by overloading a container with compressed air, are mechanical explosives

9. The alphanumeric coding of a fingerprint is a systematic description of the main patterns on the print. Within a certain metropolitan district, 90% of the population have fingerprints that can be alphanumerically coded.

   From the information given above, it can be validly concluded that the fingerprints of a person from this district, selected at random,

   A) can be alphanumerically coded, with a probability of 10%
   B) can be alphanumerically coded, with a probability of less than 90%
   C) cannot be alphanumerically coded, with a probability of 10%
   D) cannot be alphanumerically coded, with a probability of up to 90%
   E) may be coded alphanumerically, but the probability is unknown

10. The printed output of some computer-driven printers can be recognized by forensic analysts. The "Acme Model 200" printer was manufactured using two different inking mechanisms, one of which yields a "Type A" micropattern of ink spray around its characters. Of all Acme Model 200 printers, 70% produce this Type A micropattern, which is also characteristic of some models of other printers. Forensic analysts at a crime lab have been examining a kidnap ransom note which clearly exhibits the Type A micropattern.

    From the information given above, it can be validly concluded that this note

    A) was printed on an Acme Model 200 printer, with a probability of 70%
    B) was printed on an Acme Model 200 printer, with a probability of 30%
    C) was not printed on an Acme Model 200 printer, with a probability of 70%
    D) was not printed on an Acme Model 200 printer, with a probability of 30%
    E) may have been printed on an Acme Model 200 printer, but the probability cannot be estimated

Analysis of Logical Reasoning Practice Test Questions

1. Correct Answer:
B) some jurisdictions still distinguish between crimes *malum in se* and *malum prohibitum*

This question is concerned with classification of crimes into sets—that is, with the classification of crimes as either *malum in se* or *malum prohibitum*. The last phrase in the last sentence tells us that many jurisdictions make the distinction between these two categories of crimes. Response B follows from that sentence, because if many jurisdictions make the distinction, some jurisdictions make the distinction. From the fact that many jurisdictions make the distinction, it cannot be inferred that many do not make the distinction. Therefore, Response A is incorrect.

Responses C, D, and E are based on erroneous definitions of the two classes of crimes. The paragraph tells us that all crimes characterized as *malum in se* are inherently evil. Response C is false because it cannot be the case that SOME crimes characterized as *malum in se* are NOT inherently evil. The paragraph also tells us that all crimes characterized as *malum prohibitum* are declared as offenses by a legislature. Response D is false because it cannot be the case that SOME crimes characterized as *malum prohibitum* are NOT declared by a legislature to be an offense. In the paragraph, we are told that filing a tax return late is *malum prohibitum*, rather than *malum in se*. Response E is incorrect because it cannot be the case that failing to file a tax return is *malum in se*.

2. Correct Answer:
C) If Claus Inc. can show that it was not negligent, then it is not liable

The second sentence states the liability rule for common carriers: all common carriers are liable for cargo damage unless they can show that they are not negligent; if they can show that they are not negligent, then they are not liable for cargo damage. Claus Inc. is a common carrier, and accordingly this rule applies to it. From this rule it follows that if Claus Inc. can show it was not negligent, then it is not liable, Response C. Response A contradicts this rule by claiming that when Claus Inc. is liable it can show that it was not negligent. Response B contradicts this rule by claiming that Claus Inc. is not liable even when it cannot show that it is not negligent. Responses D and E concern Nichols Inc., a contract carrier. However, the terms of the Nichols Inc. contract were not disclosed in the paragraph, so neither response is supported.

3. Correct Answer:
A) some e-mail messages that have been requested as part of investigations have contained messages that would never be said face-to-face.

This is an example of a test question with a negative lead-in statement. It asks for the conclusion that is NOT supported by the paragraph. That means that four of the statements are valid conclusions from the paragraph while one is not. Response B (some messages that people would never say face-to-face are sent in e-mail messages) is a valid conclusion because it restates a fact given in the last sentence of the paragraph. Response E (some e-mail messages contain information that would be omitted from formal writing) is valid because it restates the other fact in the last sentence of the paragraph.

The next-to-last sentence in the paragraph is the source of both response C (some e-mail messages have been requested as part of investigations) and response D (e-mail messages have not been exempted from investigations). Both of these choices restate information in that sentence, based on the fact that access to e-mail messages was sought and granted. This leaves only the first option, response A (Some e-mail messages that have been requested as part of investigations have contained messages that would never be said face-to-face). This is the only choice that does NOT represent a valid conclusion, because even though we know from the paragraph that there is a group of e-mail messages that are requested in investigations and also that there is a group of messages that contain information that people would not say face-to-face, there is nothing that says that these groups overlap. We simply do not know.

4. Correct Answer:
B) Phyllis T. was not married and had no dependents.

This question concerns an either/or situation. The paragraph states that benefits under the Federal Employees Compensation Act are awarded at one level (3/4 of salary) if a beneficiary is married or has dependents when injured and at another level (2/3 of salary) if this is not true.

Phyllis T. is eligible for benefits under the Act. The paragraph states that Phyllis T.'s benefit level was 2/3 of her salary. Given this benefit level, it is clear that Phyllis T. did not meet either of the conditions for the 3/4 level. Therefore, responses A, C, and D cannot be correct (A states that she was married, C states that she had dependents, and D states that she both was married and had dependents). Response E goes beyond the facts given because prior marriages are not listed as a factor relating to this benefit. The one correct conclusion is that Phyllis T. did not meet either requirement to qualify for the higher benefit level (3/4 of salary), so response B is the correct answer to the question.

5. Correct Answer:
E) some of the engineers were immigrants

Response E is correct because it restates the third sentence in terms of the overlap between immigrants and engineers in the country described in the paragraph. Response A says that most immigrants are engineers or nurses, which are professional occupations. However, the second sentence says that most immigrants are not employed in professional occupations, so Response A is false. Response B is false because it denies that there is any overlap between immigrants and nurses, even though this overlap is clear from the third sentence of the paragraph. Response C is false because it denies the overlap between immigrants and engineers. Because the paragraph does not give complete information about the non-professionals (immigrant and non-immigrant) in the country described in the paragraph, Response D is invalid.

6. Correct Answer:
D) all of the .45 caliber weapons were sold legally

The second and last sentences are the two main premises in the paragraph. These two sentences give information about three categories of weapons: weapons made by Precision Arms, weapons sold legally, and .45 caliber weapons.

The last sentence states that none of the illegally sold weapons were .45 caliber. This means that none of the .45 caliber weapons were sold illegally. Notice that this new statement is a double negative. In affirmative form the statement means that all of the .45 caliber weapons were sold legally, Choice D.

The information that all of the .45 caliber weapons were sold legally (last sentence), combined with the information that all of the weapons made by Precision Arms were sold legally (second sentence), allows us to draw no valid conclusions about the relationship between the .45 caliber weapons and the weapons made by Precision Arms. There is insufficient information about the entire group of weapons sold legally to know whether the group of .45 caliber weapons and the group of weapons made by Precision Arms overlapped entirely (Choice A), partially (Choice C), or not at all (Choice B).

Choice E contradicts the second sentence and is, therefore, invalid.

7. Correct Answer:
C) if fingerprints are decipherable, then it is impossible to identify the person to whom they belong

This question asks for the response option that cannot be validly concluded from the information in the paragraph. The only response option that cannot be validly concluded is Response C, so the correct answer to question 7 is Response C. Response C is invalid because the paragraph does not provide enough information to conclude whether or not it would be possible to identify the person to whom the fingerprints belong from the mere fact that the fingerprints are decipherable.

Response A refers to a condition where it is possible to identify the person to whom fingerprints belong. Based on the final sentence in the paragraph, this condition of fingerprints means that the fingerprints could be classified by general shape and contour or by pattern type. Based on the second sentence, the ability to classify the fingerprints means that the fingerprints are decipherable.

Since Response B refers to a condition in which finger patterns from fingerprints are not decipherable, we know from the second sentence that, in that circumstance, they cannot be classified by general shape and contour or by pattern type. From the final sentence in the paragraph, we can infer that since they cannot be classified by these characteristics, then it is impossible to identify the person to whom the fingerprints belong.

According to the second sentence, fingerprints cannot be classified by general shape and contour or by pattern type when they are not decipherable. Therefore, if fingerprints can be classified by general shape and contour or by pattern type, then the fingerprints must be decipherable, Response D. According to the third sentence, it is impossible to identify the owner of a set of fingerprints when the fingerprints cannot be classified by general shape and contour or by pattern type. Therefore, if it is possible to identify the person to whom fingerprints belong, then the fingerprints must be able to be classified by general shape and contour or pattern type, Response E. Notice that Responses D and E are valid based on the same type of reasoning. The first and second statements of the second sentence were made opposite and reversed in Response D, and the first and second statements of the final sentence were made opposite and reversed in Response E.

8. Correct Answer:
E) some devices in which a physical reaction is produced, such as that caused by overloading a container with compressed air, are mechanical explosives

The correct answer is E. The third sentence states the overlap between all mechanical explosives and devices in which a physical reaction is produced, such as that caused by overloading a container with compressed air. From this, we can safely conclude that some devices in which a physical reaction is produced, such as that caused by overloading a container with compressed air, are mechanical explosives.

Response A is incorrect because the paragraph does not provide sufficient information to validly conclude that all explosives which have been restricted to military weapons are nuclear weapons. It may be that some types of explosives other than nuclear weapons also have been restricted to military weapons.

Responses B and C are incorrect because they contradict the paragraph. Response B contradicts the third sentence, and Response C contradicts the last sentence.

Response D is incorrect because the paragraph provides no information about whether or not mechanical explosives are restricted to military weapons.

9. Correct Answer:
C) the fingerprints of a person from this district, selected at random, cannot be alphanumerically coded, with a probability of 10%

We know from the second sentence that 90% of the people in this district have fingerprints that can be coded. Therefore, we know that 10% (100%-90%=10%) have fingerprints that cannot be coded. Given this information, the chance of selecting a person from this district with fingerprints that can be coded is 90% and the chance of selecting a person from this district with fingerprints that cannot be coded is 10%. Response A is incorrect because a probability of 10% is an underestimate of the probability that the fingerprints of a person from this district can be coded. Response B is incorrect because, like response A, it is an underestimate. Response D is incorrect because it is an overestimate of the probability that the fingerprints of a person from this district cannot be coded. Response E is incorrect because the probability that the fingerprints can be coded is known to be 90%.

10. Correct Answer: E) this note may have been printed on an Acme Model 200 printer, but the probability cannot be estimated

We know from the third sentence that the Type A micropattern exists in 70% of all Acme Model 200 printers and in some other models of printers. However, we know neither how many other models nor what percentage of other models produce the Type A micropattern. Hence, the probability that the note was printed on the Acme Model 200 printer cannot be determined. For that reason, responses A, B, C, and D are incorrect because the probability is based only on the characteristic of the one model printer that we know, the Acme Model 200, and not on all of the printer models that contain the Type A micropattern.

Section III
Arithmetic Reasoning

This section provides a quick review of basic mathematical operations and concepts that will help you answer questions on Part B -- Arithmetic Reasoning. The material in this section is in no way intended to be a complete, comprehensive guide to arithmetic. It will, however, provide a review of some of the types of mathematical functions that you must be able to perform in solving the arithmetic word problems in the test. If you have not worked on math problems for some time, you should read this information carefully before taking the arithmetic reasoning practice test. Please note that the solutions to the examples given are only one way of solving the problems. There may be other methods to reach the same right answer. And, you may find those methods to be more suitable for your way of thinking.

PREPARING FOR THE ARITHMETIC REASONING TEST

Mathematical Functions

The arithmetic reasoning questions in the test consist of math word problems that require you to perform operations such as those listed below. Examples of math problems in these areas are presented in this manual.

- Basic Addition, Subtraction, Multiplication, and Division
- Multiplication and Division of Fractions and Mixed Numbers
- Calculating Percentages
- Calculating Ratios and Proportions
- Calculating Rate Problems using Distance and Time
- Calculating Work Rate Problems
- Solving for Unknown Quantities
- Expressing Word Problems as Equations
- Calculating the Area of an Object

Whole Numbers, Fractions, and Mixed Numbers

***Quick Reminders*:**

A *whole number* is an integer (0, 1, 2, 3, 4, 5, ...) which can be divided by itself and by 1. A *fraction*, on the other hand, is a number that represents a part of a whole number. A fraction is a division or ratio of two whole numbers, written in the following form: 1/4. The top number in the fraction is called the numerator and the bottom number is referred to as the denominator.

A *mixed number* is the combination of a whole number and a fraction. For example, 9 1/4 is a mixed number which represents adding or combining the whole number "9" plus the fraction "1/4." Any mixed number can be changed into a fraction by:

- multiplying the denominator of the fraction by the whole number and adding this number to the numerator -- 4 x 9 = 36 + 1 = 37/4. This says that 9 1/4 is the same as 37/4.

Adding and Subtracting Fractions:

- To add or subtract fractions that have the same (common) denominator, add or subtract the numerators and retain the denominator:

  Example 1. 5/8 + 6/8 = 11/8. Expressed as a mixed number it is 1 3/8.

  Example 2. 4/5 - 1/5 = 3/5

- To add or subtract fractions that do not have the same denominators, first find a common denominator, then add or subtract the numerators. The least common denominator (LCD) is the smallest number into which each of the original denominators can be divided evenly. Study the example below:

  Example 3. 1/3 + 1/2 + 3/4 = ?

  In this problem, the LCD for the three fractions is 12 because 12 is the smallest number into which the numbers 3, 2, and 4 can each be divided evenly. Although 24 also is a common denominator for these three fractions, it is not the smallest denominator.

  Divide the original denominators (3, 2, and 4) of each fraction into the common denominator (12) and multiply the result for each fraction by the numerator of each fraction.

  Following these rules for the first fraction, we divide the original denominator (which is 3) into 12 (the LCD), which equals 4; 4 x 1 (the numerator) equals 4. So, the first fraction becomes 4/12.

  Repeating this operation, the second fraction becomes 6/12, and the third becomes 9/12. So, 4/12 + 6/12 + 9/12 = 19/12. Expressed as a mixed number, this becomes 1 7/12.

  Example 4. 4/5 - 1/3 = 12/15 - 5/15 = 7/15

Multiplying Fractions:

- To multiply fractions, multiply the numerators, then multiply the denominators.

  Example 5. 3/7 x 2/4 = 6/28. Reduced to its lowest term, this becomes 3/14.

Dividing Fractions:

- To divide a fraction by another fraction, invert the second fraction, and multiply the numerators and denominators.

  Example 6. 5/8 ÷ 3/4 = 5/8 x 4/3 = 20/24. Reduced to its lowest terms, this becomes 5/6.

Working with Decimals

A decimal is a fraction that is expressed in another form. Numbers that begin with a period (called a decimal point) are decimals (also called decimal fractions). For example, the numbers .75, .045, and .009 are decimals. The decimal .75 represents the fraction 3/4. If you divide the denominator (4) into the numerator (3), the result will be .75.

Adding and Subtracting Decimals:

Example 7. .35 + .78 can also be written as

$$\begin{array}{r} .35 \\ +\ .78 \\ \hline 1.13 \end{array}$$

Example 8. .69 - .14 = .55 or

$$\begin{array}{r} .69 \\ -\ .14 \\ \hline .55 \end{array}$$

Notice that the decimal points are aligned and that in the sum, the whole number is placed to the left of the decimal point.

Multiplying Decimals:

To multiply decimals, you do not need to align the decimal points. Instead, you must count the number of decimal places (to the right of the decimal point) in each set of numbers and add them. After you multiply the two sets of numbers, place the decimal point at the number of places you counted.

Example 9. 6.021 x .4 = 6021 x 4 = 24084;

Since there are 3 decimal places in 6.021 and 1 decimal place in .4, the total number of decimal places needed in the result above (24084) is 4. So, 24084 is written as 2.4084.

Dividing Decimals:

Dividing decimals also requires you to count the number of decimal places.

Example 10. In calculating 2.64 ÷ .02, it will be easier to first move the decimal point 2 places to the right in each set of numbers. This will give you 264 ÷ 2, which is equal to 132.

Check: multiplying 132 x .02 = 2.64

Example 11. 25.164 ÷ .06 = 2516.4 ÷ 6 = 419.4

Check: multiplying 419.4 x .06 = 25.164

Notice that the decimal point was moved 2 places to the right in each set of numbers above.

Word Problems Using Decimals:

Example 12. Cargo weighing 6,520 tons arrived at the Marin Port and was assessed a fee of 6 cents per ton. What was the total amount assessed on the cargo?

6 cents = .06; 6,520 x .06 = 391.20. So, the answer is $391.20.

Example 13. If inspection stickers cost 30 cents each, how many stickers can be purchased for $12.60?

30 cents = .30; 12.60 ÷ .30 = 42. So, the answer is 42.

You can also calculate this problem by moving the decimals in each set of numbers two places to the right and then dividing:

1260 ÷ 30 = 42

Percentages

A percentage is yet another way of expressing a fraction. Percentages (or percents) are expressed as fractions or parts of a whole. Writing 100% is the same as writing the fraction 100/100, and writing 23% is the same as 23/100.

- To find a percent of a number, change the percent to a decimal and multiply by the decimal:

  Example 14. 16% of 40 = 40 x .16 = 6.40

- To calculate what percent one number is of another number, reverse the calculation above and divide:

Example 15. What percent of 40 is 6.40 (also expressed as 6.40 is what percent of 40)?

Calculate 6.40 ÷ 40 = .16; move the decimal 2 places to the right in .16 to get 16%.

Calculating Percentages, Percentage Increases, and Percentage Decreases:

Example 16. Agent Crawford provided government prosecutors with 400 documents for potential use in a trial. If 18% of the documents were actually used in the trial, how many documents were used?

400 x .18 = 72. So, 72 documents were used.

Example 17. Each year an office was allocated funds to provide bonuses to all of its employees. One year, the office received the same amount of bonus funds, but lost 10% of its staff. By what percentage will the bonus amounts increase for the remaining staff in that office?

One way to solve the problem is to let 100% represent the total staff in the office. 100% - 10% = 90%. If the bonus funds previously given to the 10% of employees who left were divided among those who remained, you would get .10 ÷ .90 = .111 (11.1% or rounded to 11%). So, the bonus amounts for the remaining staff would increase by 11%.

Example 18. In June 1997, the number of investigators employed full-time in one large office was 800. One year later, that number increased 15%. What was the total number of investigators employed in the office in June 1998?

There are two ways to solve this problem. One way is to multiply 800 x .15 = 120; then add 120 + 800 = 920.

Another, quicker way is to multiply 800 x 1.15 = 920. The number 1.15 is used because the investigator workforce increased from 100% to an additional 15%, totaling 115%. Converting 115% to a decimal is expressed as 1.15.

Had the investigator workforce decreased 15% from June 1997 to June 1998, the calculation would have been 800 x .85 = 680. (Note that the decimal .85 is used because 100% minus 15% equals 85%, expressed as .85 in decimal form.) This is the same as multiplying 800 x .15 = 120 and subtracting 800 - 120 = 680.

Solving for Unknown Values

Some math problems will have missing or unknown values that you must determine or calculate in order to solve the problem. To solve a math problem that has one or more unknown (not given) values, set up an equation to represent all of the values in the problem, substituting a letter of the alphabet, such as *a*, *b*, *x*, or *y*, for the unknown value.

Example 19. A passenger purchased a vase from an art dealer in Europe for $1,210. She later learned that the dealer sold her the vase for 110% of its actual value. What was the actual value of the vase?

First, think carefully about what you need to find in order to solve the problem. In this problem, you want to find the actual value of the vase (the unknown value). Do this by substituting ***X*** for the actual value. Since the vase was sold for \$1,210 and \$1,210 is 110% of its actual value, the equation should look like the following:

$$\$1{,}210 = 110\% \text{ of } X\text{; this is also written as } \$1{,}210 = 110\%X \text{ or } 1.10X$$

This is also the same as $1.10X = 1{,}210$. Move your known values to the right side of the equation by dividing each side of the equation by 1.10; $1.10X \div 1.10 = 1{,}210 \div 1.10$.

The equation then becomes $X = 1{,}210 \div 1.10$, which is equal to 1,100 or \$1,100. Therefore, the actual value of the vase is \$1,100.

> A general rule to remember is: If you add or subtract the same value to or from each side of an equation, the new equation is equal to the original equation. If you multiply or divide both sides of an equation by the same non-zero value, the new equation is equal to the original equation. In Example 19, both sides of the equation were divided by 1.10.

Example 20. An investigator rented a car for six days and was charged \$450. The car rental company charged \$35 per day plus \$.30 per mile driven. How many miles did the investigator drive the car?

The answer can be obtained by letting X represent the number of miles driven and computing the following:

$$6\,(35) + .30X = 450$$

$$210 + .30X = 450; \quad .30X = 450 - 210; \text{ so, } .30X = 240;$$

$$\text{and, } X = 240 \div .30 = 800 \text{ (He drove 800 miles).}$$

The investigator rented the car for six days at \$35 per day, which is \$210; \$210 subtracted from the total charge of \$450 leaves \$240, the portion of the total charge expended for the miles driven. This amount divided by the charge per mile (\$240/.30) gives the number of miles (800) driven by the investigator.

Ratios and Proportions

A ratio expresses the comparison of two or more things. It indicates the amount of one thing you have compared to the amount of another thing you have.

Example 21. If you have purchased season tickets to the 2002 football games and tickets for the 2002 ballet season in the ratio of 5:3, then you have 5 football tickets for every 3 ballet tickets you purchased. Notice that this does not tell you the actual number of either set of tickets you purchased--just that you bought the tickets in the ratio indicated.

The following example shows a ratio used in a proportion:

Example 22. An investigator maintained an inventory of 500 case files for use in documenting the investigation of a large corporation. Two hundred files relating to trade compliance violations were stored in the Southeast Office, and the remaining files linking the corporation to money laundering activities were stored in the Palmer Park Office and the West Canal Street Office in the ratio of 2:3. How many files were stored at the Palmer Park Office and how many were stored at the West Canal Street Office?

The ratio of 2 to 3 tells us that out of every 5 case files, 2 will be stored in the Palmer Park Office and 3 will be stored in the West Canal Street Office. Two out of 5 has the same meaning as the fraction 2/5 or the decimal quantity .40; 3 of 5 is the same as the fraction 3/5 or .60. Since we are told that 200 of the 500 files are stored in the Southeast Office, this leaves 300 files that are stored either in the Palmer Park or West Canal Street Office. To determine how many files were stored at the Palmer Park Office, we set up the proportion $2/5 = X/300$. To solve for X, we cross multiply the two fractions and obtain $5X = (2)(300)$. Solving for X, we obtain the answer 120. Thus, 120 of the files were stored at the Palmer Park Office, and the remainder (300 - 120 = 180) were stored at the West Canal Street Office.

Solving Distance, Time, and Rate Problems

Some math problems require you to calculate the *rate* at which an event or action occurs. Review the following:

Example 23. An investigator drove 300 miles in 5 hours. At what rate (of speed) did the investigator drive? Using the formula, ***Rate = Distance ÷ Time***, 300 ÷ 5 hrs = 60 miles per hour. So, the investigator drove at a rate (speed) of 60 miles per hour.

In another version of the problem, you are given the rate and distance, but must calculate the *amount of time* it takes to travel the distance:

Example 24. An investigator traveled 300 miles at a speed of 60 mph. How long did it take the investigator to drive this distance? Using the formula, ***Time = Distance ÷ Rate***, the time it took to drive was 300 ÷ 60 mph, which is equal to 5 hrs.

Another variation provides the rate and time, but asks you to calculate the *distance*:

Example 25. An investigator traveled 5 hours at a speed of 60 mph, how many miles did the investigator travel? Using the formula, ***Distance* = *Rate*** x ***Time***, the distance driven by the investigator was 60 mph x 5 hrs, which equals 300 miles.

Now study the following example:

Example 26. If Agent Davis drove 520 miles in 8 hours, how long would it take her to drive 650 miles at the same rate?

Express the problem as 520 ÷ 8 = 650 ÷ X, where X represents the amount of time it would take to drive 650 miles at the same rate of 520 miles in 8 hours (a rate of 65 mph). This becomes
520X = 650 x 8 = 5,200, and X = 5200 ÷ 520 = 10. So, it would take Agent Davis 10 hours to drive 650 miles going 65 mph.

Other variations of this type of math problem involve calculating the rate or amount of time taken to complete an assignment or task (referred to as a work rate problem). Review the examples below:

Example 27. Agent Hilton was asked to review the personal records of suspects in 5 major cases. After 2 hours, she had completed 4/7 of the records. Working at this same rate, how long will it take her to review all of the records?

This problem is solved using the same basic formula as that presented in Example 26.
4/7 X = 2 hrs., where X represents the total number of records to be reviewed. The problem becomes X = 2 ÷ 4/7 = 2 x 7/4 = 14/4 = 3.5. So, it would take her 3.5 hrs to complete the entire task.

Example 28. Four employees were asked to stack 320 boxes of materials. After stacking 120 boxes in 1 hour, they were joined by another worker who helped stack the remaining boxes. How long will it take the new group to finish stacking the remaining 200 boxes, if they continue to work at their same rate?

In this problem you must first determine how many boxes are being stacked by the four employees in one hour (120 boxes per hour ÷ 4 employees = 30 boxes per hour per employee). Continuing at the same rate, 5 individuals would stack 150 boxes per hour (5 employees x 30 boxes = 150 boxes). Subtracting 150 from 200 leaves 50 boxes that remain to be stacked after 1 hour. The remaining 50 boxes would take an additional 1/3 hour to stack since 50 boxes ÷ 150 (the number stacked in 1 hour) = 1/3. Therefore, the total time it would take the 5 employees to stack the remaining 200 boxes would be 1 1/3 hours.

OR algebraically speaking: Since 4 employees stack 120 boxes per hour, each employee stacks an average of 30 boxes per hour (see Part A below). To find the amount of time it would take for 5 workers, working at the same pace, to stack 200 remaining boxes, use the formula in Part B below, where x is the unknown time in hours.

Part A

(1) $120 = 4x$

(2) $\frac{120}{4} = \frac{4x}{4}$

(3) $30 = x$

Part B

(1) $200 = 5(30x)$

(2) $200 = 150x$

(3) $\frac{200}{150} = \frac{150x}{150}$

(4) $1.33 = x$

Expressing Word Problems as Equations

Some of the word problems in the test require you to choose, from among several equations, the one equation that expresses or represents a solution to the problem. Review the example below:

Example 29. An agency purchased surplus computer printers for $220 each. For every 20 printers purchased, the twentieth printer received a 40% discount. What equation represents the total price paid, if the agency purchased 100 of the printers?

The equation would be: 100 (220) - [(100/20 x (220)) x .40]

The total price of the computers, without the discount, is represented by 100 (220) = $22,000. The number of printers that were purchased at a discount (every 20th computer) is represented by 100/20, which equals 5. So, the cost of 5 printers priced at $220 is represented by 100/20 (220). A 40% discount for this price is represented by 100/20 (220) times .40, the results of which must be subtracted from $22,000 to obtain the total discounted price paid by the agency.

Note that this type of problem does not require you to actually solve the problem. Instead, you are asked only to find the one equation, from among a choice of four equations, that represents the correct way to solve the problem.

Final Tips: Review of Basic Formulas and Measures

Some questions in the test will require you to work with the elements of time (hours and minutes) and certain types of measures (length, width, and area of a square or rectangle). It will be useful to remember the following basics:

60 seconds = 1 minute
60 minutes = 1 hour
24 hours = 1 day
Area = L x W (the area of a square or rectangle is obtained by multiplying its length times its width)
Rate = Distance divided by Time (R = D/T)
Time = Distance divided by Rate (T = D/R)
Distance = Rate multiplied by Time (D = R x T)

ARITHMETIC REASONING PRACTICE TEST

In this part of the test you will have to solve problems formulated in both verbal and numeric form. You will have to analyze a paragraph in order to set up the problem, and then solve it. If the exact answer is not given as one of the response choices, you should select response E, "none of these." Some of the questions in the actual test will be easier and some will be harder than the ones in this practice test.

1. Agent Y was asked to conduct a detailed interview with a suspect. After 2 hours, the agent had completed 4/9 of the interview. Continuing at this same rate, how long did it take Agent Y to complete the entire interview?

   A) 3.5 hrs
   B) 4 hrs
   C) 4.5 hrs
   D) 5 hrs
   E) none of these

2. Agent Phelps and Agent Mabry reviewed and approved case files involving smuggling activities for several area offices. Of the 190 records they reviewed together, Agent Phelps approved 3 cases for every 2 approved by Agent Mabry. How many cases did Agent Mabry approve?

   A) 38
   B) 76
   C) 114
   D) 285
   E) none of these

3. An investigator drove east at an average speed of 90 kilometers (km) per hour for 3 minutes. During the remaining 100 minutes of her travel, the investigator drove north. If the investigator drove a total of 204.5 km, what was her average speed when traveling north?

   A) 95 km/hr
   B) 100 km/hr
   C) 120 km/hr
   D) 130 km/hr
   E) none of these

4. While working the evening shift, Agent K took 8 hours to complete a task and Agent M took 10 hours to complete the same type of task. How many hours would it take Agent K and Agent M to complete the same task working together, each working at his own rate?

   A) 9
   B) 8 1/9
   C) 4 4/9
   D) 6 3/4
   E) none of these

5. An investigator traveling on official business in his personal vehicle had to make emergency repairs to the vehicle. He paid $150 for the repairs plus 15% of this amount to compensate the mechanic for repair work performed overtime. The investigator's office reimbursed him $100 plus 40% of any amount over $100. Which one of the equations below represents the amount that the investigator was reimbursed for the repairs?

   A) $100 + .4 [150 (1.15) - 100] = X$
   B) $4 [(150) (.15) + 100] = X$
   C) $100 + (150) (.15) = X$
   D) $150 + .4 [150 (1.15) - 100] = X$
   E) none of these

6. Agent Jordyn had to count 13,000 dollar bills by hand. Agents Terri and Stewart were assigned to help. After 1 hour, Agent Stewart had counted 1,000 bills, but had to leave for firearms training. Working at their same rate, how long will it take Agents Jordyn and Terri to count the remaining 9,000 bills?

   A) 1 hr, 15 mins
   B) 2 hrs, 15 mins
   C) 2 hrs, 45 mins
   D) 3 hrs
   E) none of these

7. The administrative assistant at a law enforcement training academy purchases badges priced at $32 each for all the graduates of the academy. The last training class graduated 25 new officers. What is the total amount of money the academy will spend for the badges for these new officers, if the badge vendor provides the Academy a 20% discount on each badge?

   A) $ 800
   B) $ 790
   C) $ 640
   D) $ 16
   E) none of these

Solutions to the Arithmetic Reasoning Questions

1. **Correct Answer: C** — Agent Y completed one segment of the interview, that is, 4/9 of the interview, in 2 hours. One compete interview can be divided into 2 1/4 segments, 1 ÷ 4/9 = 9/4 = 2 1/4. We can multiply the number of segments, 2 1/4, by the number of hours each segment takes to complete, 2, in order to calculate the number of hours to complete the entire interview: 2 1/4 x 2 = 4 1/2.

2. **Correct Answer: B** — The ratio 3:2 means that for every 5 approvals, 3 will be done by Agent Phelps and 2 by Agent Mabry. Agent Phelps approved 3/5 x 190; Agent Mabry approved 2/5 x 190 = 76.

3. **Correct Answer: C** — 3 mins = 1/20 hr (60 ÷3); 1/20 x 90 km/hr = 4.5 km traveled in the first 3 minutes; 204.5 km - 4.5 km = 200 km remaining.
100 mins = 1 hour and 40 minutes which equals 1 2/3 hrs or 5/3 hrs; speed (rate) for the remaining 200 km = 200 km ÷ 5/3 hrs = 120 km/hr

4. **Correct Answer: C** — Let Agent K's hours be represented by 1/8 and Agent M's hours be represented by 1/10. This says that Agent K completes 1/8 of the job per hour and Agent M completes 1/10 of the job per hour. Together, they work 1/8 + 1/10 = 18/80 of the job per hour, which when reduced to its lowest terms, is 9/40. Therefore, if **T** is the amount of time it takes the two of them to finish the job, then 9/40 of the job per hour x **T** (hours) has to equal 1 job. So, 9/40 x **T** = 1 and **T** = 40/9 = 4 4/9 hours (four and four-ninths hours).

5. **Correct Answer: A** — 100 + .4 [150 (1.15) - 100] = X

6. **Correct Answer: D** — The Agents began with 13,000 bills to count, and when Agent Stewart left, there were 9,000 bills remaining. This means that the 3 Agents working together for one hour counted 4,000 bills, 13,000 - 9,000 = 4,000. Agent Stewart counted 1,000 of the 4,000 bills counted, so the other 2 Agents counted 3,000 bills in one hour. The remaining 9,000 bills can be divided evenly into 3 groups of 3,000 bills, 9,000 ÷ 3,000 = 3. Since it takes the 2 Agents 1 hour to review 3,000 bills, it will take them 3 hours to review the remaining bills, 1hour x 3 groups of bills = 3 hours to count the remaining bills.

7. **Correct Answer: C** — $32 x 25 = 800; 800 x .20 = 160; $800 - 160 = $640. The second way to calculate the answer is: $800 x .80 = $640.

SECTION IV
WRITING SKILLS ASSESSMENT

This guide has been developed to help you prepare for the Writing Skills Assessment.

This guide provides information that will refresh your knowledge of some basic rules of English grammar, syntax, usage, sentence and paragraph organization, and punctuation. Only a short summary of each topic is provided. For a more in-depth study, you may want to refer to English textbooks or writing handbooks. A reference list with some suggested readings is provided. Also, this guide presents a sample of the types of questions you can expect to find on the Writing Skills Test along with the correct answers and the rationale for them.

PREPARING FOR THE WRITING SKILLS ASSESSMENT

Sentence Construction

- A sentence is a grammatically independent group of words that serves as a unit of expression.

- A sentence normally contains a stated *subject* (the noun(s) and/or pronoun(s) the sentence is about), and it must contain a *predicate* (the part that says something about or directs the subject) that consists of at least one word, a verb. Even the single-word command *Go!* is a sentence because it has an unstated but implied subject – whoever or whatever is being directed to go – and a verb.

Use of Phrases in Sentences

- A phrase is a group of related words lacking a subject and/or a predicate. A phrase can be used as a noun, adjective, adverb, or verb. On the basis of their form, phrases are classified as *prepositional*, *participial*, *gerund*, *infinitive*, and *verb* phrases.

Use of Clauses in Sentences

- Clauses are grammatical units containing a subject and a verb. They can be either dependent or independent. An independent clause expresses the main thought of the sentence and can stand alone as a sentence (**Example:** She laughed.). A dependent clause expresses an idea that is less important than the idea expressed in the main clause and cannot stand alone as a sentence (**Example:** As she was laughing…).

Restrictive and Nonrestrictive Phrases and Clauses

- A *restrictive* phrase or clause provides information that is necessary to specifically identify what is being described. A *nonrestrictive* phrase or clause provides information that is incidental to the meaning of the sentence.

- Generally speaking, restrictive phrases and clauses are not separated from the rest of the sentence by commas. Nonrestrictive phrases and clauses are separated from the rest of the sentence by commas.

Examples: The blue house that he built on a hill is quite large.
The blue house, which he built on a hill, is quite large.

The first sentence is written about a man who built several blue houses but only one on a hill. Therefore, the phrase *that he built on a hill* is essential for knowing which blue house is being referred to. The phrase is therefore restrictive and is not separated from the rest of the sentence by commas.

The second example is written about a man who built only one blue house, and it happens to be on a hill. Therefore, *which he built on a hill* is not essential for knowing which house is being referred to. The phrase is therefore nonrestrictive and is separated from the rest of the sentence by commas.

Examples: We should congratulate the student who won the prize.
Pat, who won the prize, deserves our congratulations.

In the first sentence the clause *who won the prize* is essential for indicating the person who should be congratulated. The clause is therefore restrictive and is not separated from the rest of the sentence by commas.

In the second sentence, the person to be congratulated is identified as Pat, and the clause *who won the prize* is not essential for identifying the person. The clause is therefore nonrestrictive and is separated from the rest of the sentence by commas.

Verb

Definition: A word or phrase used to assert an action or state of being.

Verb Voice

- The *voice* of a verb shows whether the subject performs an action (active voice) or receives it (passive voice).
  Example (active voice): The consultant wrote a proposal.
  Example (passive voice): The proposal was written by the consultant.

Verb Tense

- The tense of a verb shows the time of the action of the verb. There are an active and a passive form of all tenses in English. The six English verb tenses are:

Tense	*Examples of Active Voice*	*Examples of Passive Voice*
Present	she takes; she is taking	she is taken; she is being taken
Past	she took; she was taking	she was taken; she was being taken
Future	she will take; she will be taking	she will be taken
Present perfect	she has taken; she has been taking	she has been taken
Past perfect	she had taken; she had been taking	she had been taken
Future perfect	she will have taken; she will have been taking	she will have been taken

- The *present* tense represents action that is taking place now.
  Example: She *is attending* training today.

- The *past* tense represents action that took place in past time.
  Example: He *wrote* five letters yesterday.

- The *future* tense places action in future time.
  Example: She *will attend* the meeting later today.

- The *present perfect* tense represents action completed before the present time.
  Example: He *has taken* training.

- The *past perfect* tense represents action that occurs before another past action.
  Example: She counted the letters he *had written.*

- The *future perfect* tense represents action that will be completed before a specific time in the future.
  Example: By next week, he *will have completed* the analysis.

Verb Mood

- The *mood* of a verb shows whether an action is fact (indicative mood), something other than fact, such as a possibility, wish, or supposition (subjunctive mood), or a command (imperative mood).
  Example of indicative mood: They *are going* to the ball game.
  Example of subjunctive mood: I insist that he *go* to the ball game.
  Example of imperative mood: *Go* now!

- The subjunctive mood is also used to express a condition contrary to fact.
  Example: I wish I *were* president.

Other Rules Related to Verbs

- Transitive verbs require direct objects to complete their meaning.
  Example: The baseball player *signed the autographs.*

- Intransitive verbs do not require direct objects to complete their meaning.
  Example: The boat *has docked.*

- Linking verbs are not action verbs; rather, they express a state of being or existence. The various forms of the verb *to be* are primary linking verbs.

- Linking verbs never take objects but, instead, connect the subject to a word or idea in the predicate. **Examples:** It *was* he who bought the tickets. His proposal *is* unacceptable. Some dogs *are* excitable.

- The verb *to be* can also be used with another verb as a helping (auxiliary) verb to create a verb phrase. **Examples:** Flights *have been delayed.* The contract will *have to be reviewed.*

Infinitive

Definition: An infinitive is the form of a verb that expresses action or existence without reference to person, number, or tense. **Example:** *To run* is relaxing.

- A split infinitive has a word or several words between the *to* and the *verb* following it. Splitting an infinitive is generally considered incorrect, especially if more than one word intervenes between *to* and the verb. **Incorrect example:** You should try *to*, if you can, *attend* the briefing. **Correct usage:** You should try *to attend* the briefing, if you can.

- An infinitive may be used as the subject of a sentence. **Example:** *To become* champion has been her lifelong dream.

- An infinitive may be used as an adjectival modifier. **Example:** He had several papers *to review* during the trip.

Gerund

Definition: A gerund is the form of a verb ending in *ing* that is used as a noun. In fact, another name for a gerund is a verbal noun.

- A gerund may be used as the subject of a sentence. **Example:** *Drawing* was his favorite personal activity.

- A gerund may be used as the object of a sentence or a prepositional phrase.
  Example: She preferred *walking* over *bicycling. Walking* is the object of the verb *preferred* and *bicycling* is the object of the preposition *over*.

Participle

Definition: A participle is a form of the verb used as an adjective. Simple participle forms end in *ed* or *ing*. **Examples:** The candidate felt *betrayed.* The New Year's Eve party was *exciting.*

- When a participial phrase seems to modify a word that it cannot sensibly modify, then it is a dangling phrase. **Incorrect example:** Sailing on the open sea, many dolphins were spotted. (*Sailing* does not modify dolphins.) **Correct usage:** Sailing on the open sea, we spotted many dolphins.

Noun

Definition: A noun is a word that names a person, place, thing, quality, idea, or action.

- A common noun identifies one or more of a class of persons, places, things, qualities, ideas, or actions that are alike. **Examples:** The girl chained her *bicycle* to the *fence.*
- A proper noun identifies a particular person, place, thing, quality, idea, or action. (*Note*: Proper nouns must be capitalized.) **Examples:** *Joe Brown* drove his *Lincoln Towncar* to the *Kennedy Center.*
- A collective noun identifies a group of people or things that are related or acting as one. **Examples:** The *jury* arrives at the courthouse each day at nine in the morning. The *platoon* travels by night in order to avoid detection. Collective nouns are *single* in number; thus, they take a singular verb.
    - If the individual members of the group are referred to, then the plural verb can be used. **Example:** A group of employees *are* sharing supplies with each other.
- The possessive of a singular noun is formed by adding an apostrophe and *s* to the noun. **Examples:** the boy's sweater; Alice's car
- The possessive of a plural noun ending in *s* is formed by adding an apostrophe only. **Examples:** agents' salaries; workers' union

Pronoun

Definition: A pronoun is a word that is used in place of a noun, most frequently to eliminate monotonous repetition of the noun. There are nine types of pronouns:

- Demonstrative pronouns point out a specific person or thing. **Examples:** this, that, these, those
- Indefinite pronouns refer to people or things generally rather than specifically. **Examples:** all, any, anybody, anyone, anything, both, each, either, everybody, everyone, everything, few, many, most, much, neither, no one, nobody, none, nothing, one, other, several, some, somebody, someone, something, such
- Verbs used with indefinite pronouns must agree with the pronoun in number.

Examples: none *is*; much *is*; everyone *is*; many *are*

- *None* is generally used in a singular sense. If you think of *none* as *no one person or thing*, then it is easy to see that it is singular in meaning and takes a singular verb. However, when *none* is used in the sense of *not two* or *no amount*, then a plural verb is used. **Example:** None of the team members are in agreement.

- Interrogative pronouns are used to ask questions. **Examples:** who, what, which

- Relative pronouns relate a subordinate part of a sentence to the main clause. **Examples:** who, whoever, whom, whomever, whose, which, whichever, what, that

  - *Who* and *whoever* are used as subjects in a sentence or phrase, while *whom* and *whomever* are used as objects in a sentence or phrase. **Examples:** *Who* will get the tickets? *Whoever* is going will buy the tickets. I need to give tickets to *whom*? The tickets will be given to *whomever* I see first.

- Personal pronouns refer to persons or things and change form in three different persons: first person (the person speaking), second person (the person spoken to), and third person (person or thing spoken about).

  - First person pronouns: I, we (used as subject of sentences and clauses) me, us (used as objects of verbs and prepositions)

  - Second person pronoun: you (used for singular and plural, for subjects and objects)

  - Third person pronouns: he, she, it they (used as subject of sentences and clauses)
    him, her, it, them (used as objects of verbs and prepositions)

  Examples: Bill and *I* are going. She told Sally and *me*.

- Possessive pronouns determine ownership or possession without using an apostrophe followed by an *s*. **Examples:** my, mine, our, ours, yours, his, hers, its, their, theirs (*Note*: *it's* is not a personal pronoun; it is the contraction of *it is*.)

- Reflexive pronouns refer back to the pronoun used as the subject of the sentence. **Examples:** I burned *myself*. You are deceiving *yourself*.

- Intensive pronouns are used to emphasize the first pronoun. **Examples:** You *yourself* must register. I *myself* do not understand.

Adjective and Adverb

Definitions: An adjective is a word that modifies a noun. An adverb is a word that modifies a verb, an adjective, or another adverb.

- An adjective or an adverb should be placed so that there is no doubt as to which word it modifies. **Example:** The *angry* boy *quickly* threw the ball. *Angry* is an adjective modifying the noun *boy*. *Quickly* is an adverb modifying the verb *threw*.

- Adjectives and adverbs show degrees of quality or quantity by means of their positive, comparative, and superlative forms. The positive form expresses no comparison at all. The comparative form adds an *-er* to the positive form of the adjective or adverb or prefixes the positive form with the word *more* to express a greater degree or a comparison between two persons or things. The superlative form adds an *-est* to the positive form of the adjective or adverb or prefixes the positive form with the word *most* to express the greatest degree of quantity or quality among three or more persons or things.

  Examples:

Positive	**Comparative**	**Superlative**
short	shorter	shortest
beautiful	more beautiful	most beautiful
big	bigger	biggest
hard	harder	hardest

- Many adverbs have the characteristic *ly* ending. **Example:** quickly, slowly, angrily

Article

Definition: An article is a word that refers to a noun and gives definiteness or indefiniteness to the noun.

- The English articles are *a, an*, and *the*.

  - *A* and *an* are the indefinite articles. They are used for general nouns or when the audience does not know which thing you are referring to. *A* is used before words that begin with a consonant, and *an* is used before words that begin with a vowel. **Examples**: *An* attorney will meet you today. *A* file is missing from my desk.

  - *The* is the definite article. It is used when the audience knows which thing is being referred to. **Example**: *The* attorney that you met with last week has returned your call.

Preposition

Definition: A preposition is a word that connects a noun to some other word in the sentence. Prepositions usually establish a relationship of time or location. The use of a preposition automatically creates a prepositional phrase. **Examples:** *in* a month; *after* a year; *on* the table; *behind* the door

- There are over 40 prepositions in English, some of which are: *about, around, before, at, below, by, for, from, in, of, on, to, through, up, upon,* and *with.*

Conjunction

Definition: A conjunction (also known as a connective) is a word that joins together sentences, clauses, phrases, or words.

- Conjunctions that connect two or more parts of a sentence that are of equal rank (Example: two nouns or verbs or phrases, etc.) are called coordinating conjunctions. **Examples:** *and, but, or, nor, for,* and sometimes *yet*

- Subordinating conjunctions connect dependent (subordinate) clauses to independent (main) clauses. Subordinating conjunctions include *though, if, as, when, while,* and *since*.
  Example: *Since he took the course for his own advancement*, his employer wouldn't pay for it.

- Correlative conjunctions are pairs of words that connect sentence elements that are of equal rank. Correlative conjunctions must always appear together in the same sentence. **Examples:** *either-or, neither-nor, whether-or, both-and,* and *not only-but also*

  Examples used in sentences:
  Neither the manager *nor* the employee had a reasonable solution to the problem.
  Whether he stayed home *or* went to work depended on a change in his symptoms.
  Both the program office *and* the budget office agreed on the increase in funding for the new equipment.
  She was outstanding *not only* in her academic coursework *but also* in her fitness training.

Avoiding Verb, Noun, and Pronoun Shifts

- Unnecessary shifts in person, number, tense, or voice confuse readers and seriously weaken communication. The examples below indicate these types of errors.

- A shift in person occurs when a writer shifts back and forth among the first, second, and third persons. **Incorrect example:** If *you* want to pass the physical, *a person* has to exercise daily.

- A shift in number occurs when a plural pronoun is used to refer back to a singular antecedent or vice versa. **Incorrect example:** *Anyone* who shops in that department store must seriously consider *their* budget.

- Unnecessary shifts in tense more commonly occur within a paragraph rather than within an individual sentence. **Incorrect example:** After the historian *spent* several hours describing the armies' strategies, he *gave* a horrifying account of the attack. He *points* out in great detail what *is* going on in the minds of each of the soldiers.
- A shift in voice occurs when a writer makes unnecessary shifts between the active and the passive voice. **Incorrect example:** *I wrote* the journal article; the *book chapter was*

also *written* by me. (In this example, the first clause is active voice and the second shifts to passive voice.)

- When two sentence elements are joined by a conjunction, they should have parallel structure.
  Correct example: She was outstanding not only *in her academic coursework* but also *in her fitness training.*
  Incorrect example: She was outstanding not only *in her academic coursework* but also *she excelled in fitness training.*

Sentence Organization within Paragraphs

- A paragraph presents a larger unit of thought than a sentence can contain.

A paragraph must meet certain requirements:

- A paragraph should have *unity,* that is, internal consistency. It should not digress from the dominant idea expressed in the topic sentence.

- A paragraph should have *completeness.* It should present enough detailed information about the topic sentence to answer any general questions the reader may have. More specific questions would require additional paragraphs with new topic sentences.

- A paragraph should have *coherence.* Sentences should flow into each other so that the reader experiences the paragraph as an integrated unit, not as a collection of separate sentences.

- A paragraph should have *order.* Like structure in a larger work, order in a paragraph grows partly out of the material and is partly imposed by the writer. Most paragraphs and essays follow one of the two patterns that follow.

  - *From the general to the particular:* This type of paragraph begins with a topic sentence that serves as an introductory summary of the topic. The remaining sentences explain or illustrate this statement, so that the idea becomes increasingly clear as the paragraph progresses. The topic sentence is usually at or near the beginning of the paragraph.
  - *From the particular to the general*: This type of paragraph is the reverse of the previous pattern. It begins with a series of explanatory or illustrative statements that lead to a general statement or summary. The topic sentence is usually at or near the end of the paragraph.

A paragraph can be looked upon as a microcosm, an exact parallel in miniature of the entire work:

- It has a dominant idea, usually expressed in a topic sentence.

- The dominant idea is developed by examples, comparisons, explanations, or arguments to make the meaning of the topic sentence clear.
- There may be a concluding restatement of the topic idea.

Capitalization

Definition: Capitalization is the use of capital letters to place special emphasis on particular letters to set them off from lower-case letters.

- Sentences always begin with a capital letter.
- The first letter of a quotation is always capitalized.
- Proper nouns, that is, nouns that name particular persons, places, or things, must be capitalized. **Examples:** Appalachian Mountains, Mississippi River, Brooklyn Bridge
- Titles that precede a proper name are capitalized; those that follow a proper name are not. **Examples:** Chairperson John Smith and John Smith, the chairperson

Punctuation

Definition: Punctuation is the use of periods, commas, semicolons, colons, question marks, exclamation points, dashes, apostrophes, brackets, parentheses, slashes, and quotation marks to convey the pauses and gestures that we use in speech to clarify and emphasize meaning.

- Use a period to end a sentence. **Example:** She went to the beach.
- Use a period after abbreviations. **Examples:** Mr. Ms. U.S. Corp.
- Use a comma to separate independent clauses in a compound sentence. **Example:** Suzanne made a presentation at the conference, and then she spent the remainder of the day touring the city.
- Use a comma to separate an introductory phrase or clause from the main clause of a sentence. **Example:** After completing the work, the contractor left the site.
- Place a comma after every item in a series. **Example:** The new office is furnished with a desk, a computer, two chairs, and a supply cabinet.
- Two or more adjectives that modify the noun that they precede are separated by commas. **Example:** The cold, windy morning was not a good beginning for their vacation.
- Commas are used to set off the items in a date. **Example:** On Monday, August 17, 1998, he became the head of the office. Commas are not used when only the month and year are given. **Example:** August 2002

- A semicolon is used to separate elements in a series when some of the elements already contain commas. **Example:** Sally wishes us to attend the first, third, and fifth sessions on Wednesday; the second, fourth, and sixth sessions on Thursday; and the first only on Friday.

- A semicolon is used to join two closely related independent clauses that are not joined by a conjunction. **Example:** The project began slowly; thereafter, additional staff were assigned to it.

References

The Elements of Style. Strunk, Jr., W. & White, E.B. Needham Heights, MA: Allyn & Bacon, 2000. ISBN# 020530902X.

Better Sentence Writing in 30 Minutes a Day. Campbell, D. Franklin Lakes, NJ: The Career Press, Inc., 1995. ISBN# 1564142035.

Business English. Geffner, A. Hauppauge, N.Y.: Barron's Educational Services, Inc., 1998. ISBN# 0764102788.

Business Writing at Work. Davidson, E.J. Burr Ridge, IL: Irwin Mirror Press, 1994. ISBN# 0256142203.

Effective Business Writing. Piotrowski, M. New York, NY: HarperCollins, 1996. ISBN# 0062733818.

The Business Writer's Handbook. Brusaw, T., Alred, G. J. & Oliu, W.O. New York, NY: St. Martin's Press, 1993. ISBN# 0312198051.

The Classic Guide to Better Writing. Flesch, R. & Lass, A. H. New York, NY: Harper Collins, 1996. ISBN# 0062730487.

WRITING SKILLS PRACTICE TEST

For questions 1-2, select the one option that represents a change that should be made to correct the sentence. If no correction is necessary, choose option (E).

1. The U.S. Government will seek extradition of each of the defendants to the United States.

   (A) Change of each to each
   (B) Change of each to to each
   (C) Change defendants to to defendants per
   (D) Change defendants to to defendants of
   (E) No correction is necessary

2. Ms. Reece was a primary suspect, and the fraudulent credit cards were eventually traced back to she and Mr. Hanes.

   (A) Change she and Mr. Hanes to Mr. Hanes and she
   (B) Change she and Mr. Hanes to her and Mr. Hanes
   (C) Change she and Mr. Hanes to she and he
   (D) Change she and Mr. Hanes to her and he
   (E) No correction is necessary

For question 3, select the one word that completes the sentence correctly.

3. The suspect who confessed to taking the money explained that he was desperate and there was no __________ available.

   (A) substitute
   (B) alternate
   (C) decision
   (D) alternative
   (E) expedient

For question 4, select the correct spelling of the missing word.

4. Police have received more than twenty reports of _____________ bills at restaurants and grocery stores since the beginning of September.

   (A) counterfit
   (B) counterfeit
   (C) counterfet
   (D) counterfete
   (E) counterfitt

For question 5, select the one option that is correctly punctuated.

5. (A) The goods were listed on the invoice as children's clothing; however, the goods that I inspected were consumer electronics.
   (B) The goods were listed on the invoice as children's clothing; however, the goods, that I inspected, were consumer electronics.
   (C) The goods were listed on the invoice as children's clothing. However the goods that I inspected were consumer electronics.
   (D) The goods were listed on the invoice as children's clothing. However, the goods, that I inspected, were consumer electronics.

For question 6, select the one sentence that uses the correct capitalization.

6. (A) Special Agent Taylor gave a briefing today to senator Barnes on the uses of the USA Patriot act.
   (B) Special agent Taylor gave a briefing today to Senator Barnes on the uses of the USA Patriot Act.
   (C) Special Agent Taylor gave a briefing today to Senator Barnes on the uses of the USA Patriot Act.
   (D) Special Agent Taylor gave a briefing today to senator Barnes on the uses of the USA Patriot act.

For question 7, select the correct sentence order to form a paragraph that is organized, clear, and coherent. If no correction is necessary, choose option (E).

7.

(1)	Smith was arrested the following day and charged with two counts of possession and distribution of child pornography.
(2)	Agents from the Bureau of Immigration and Customs Enforcement (ICE) and the Federal Bureau of Investigations (FBI) arrested John Smith earlier this week for crimes related to child pornography.
(3)	On August 19, ICE and FBI agents executed a search warrant at the home of John Smith, seizing a computer, pornographic publications, diskettes, and documents.
(4)	If convicted, Smith could receive up to 5 years in prison and/or be required to pay fines totaling up to $100,000.

A) 4 – 3 – 2 – 1
B) 3 – 1 – 4 – 2
C) 2 – 3 – 1 – 4
D) 2 – 1 – 4 – 3
E) no correction is necessary

For question 8, select the correct order of paragraphs to create a document that is organized, clear, and coherent. If no change to the paragraph order is necessary, choose option (E).

8.

(1) Project Shield America will have two operational components. The first will be to reach out and form partnerships with U.S. manufacturers and distributors of the sensitive technology, weapons, and equipment sought by terrorists. The second will be to investigate and halt those attempting to acquire and illegally export weapons components to groups intent on harming America.

(2) Beginning immediately, field offices will identify the specific U.S. firms in their areas that manufacture or distribute materials of interest. Agents will then visit these firms and provide them with materials about Project Shield America, information about U.S. export controls, and data about the items sought by terrorists. Most importantly, the agents will encourage these firms to notify agents if they are approached by customers looking to acquire and export their products illegally.

(3) In sum, under the banner of Project Shield America, we will partner with U.S. industry to prevent their technological accomplishments from being exploited by terrorists. While some of these materials may seem relatively innocuous and have relatively little monetary value, they can have enormous strategic value in the hands of America's adversaries. These "minor" technological goods could easily become the necessary components for major weapons development by terrorist groups or rogue nations.

(4) At the same time, agents will step up their efforts to investigate and prosecute those who attempt to acquire and illegally export sensitive technology, weapons, and equipment to international terrorist organizations. These efforts will include undercover probes and other investigative techniques. The Office of Strategic Investigations will redirect its resources towards the objective of denying terrorist organizations access to these materials. Assistance from U.S. manufacturers and distributors will be crucial in this effort.

A) 1 – 4 – 2 – 3
B) 1 – 4 – 3 – 2
C) 1 – 2 – 4 – 3
D) 2 – 1 – 4 – 3
E) no correction is necessary

Answers to the Writing Skills Questions

1. **Correct Answer: E** No change to the sentence is necessary.

2. **Correct Answer: B** As the object of the preposition 'to,' the correct pronoun is 'her.'

3. **Correct Answer: D** "Alternative" means one of two possibilities and involves choice. In question three the suspect is claiming that no other choice was available.

4. **Correct Answer: B** The correct spelling is "counterfeit."

5. **Correct Answer: A** The correct answer is (A). The sentence offers correct punctuation.

6. **Correct Answer: C** The correct capitalization of the words "Special Agent Taylor, " "Senator Barnes," and "USA Patriot Act" are used in this sentence.

7. **Correct Answer: C** The most logical order of the passages is 2, 3, 1, 4. Sentence 2 uses the phrase "earlier this week" which indicates that sentence 2 should begin the paragraph. Sentence 1 refers back to a specific date, which is found in sentence 3, indicating that sentence 1 should immediately follow sentence 3. Only Response C begins with sentence 2 and orders sentence 1 immediately after sentence 3. Sentence 4 provides information which follows from the arrest mentioned in sentence 3 and serves as the conclusion to the paragraph.

8. **Correct Answer: C** The most logical order of the passages is 1, 2, 4, 3. The first paragraph introduces Project Shield America and defines the two operational components of the project. Accordingly, paragraph 1 should be the first paragraph. Paragraphs 2 and 4 elaborate on the two operational components of the project introduced in paragraph 1 and therefore must follow paragraph 1. Paragraph 2 logically comes before paragraph 4 because paragraph 2 elaborates on the first operational component of the project whereas paragraph 4 elaborates on the second operational component. Finally, paragraph 3 is clearly the concluding paragraph because it provides a summation and closing for the entire passage. The paragraphs presented in this order form a well-organized, coherent passage.

Made in the USA
Coppell, TX
30 April 2020